Introducing Julian

Woman of Norwich

D1514124

FOR MICHELE
Michael, Benjamin and Samuel
and in memory of Pearl

INTRODUCING JULIAN
Woman of Norwich

Elizabeth Ruth Obbard

Illustrated by the authoress

New City

First published in Great Britain 1995
by New City
57 Twyford Avenue, London W3 9PZ

All illustrations by Elizabeth Ruth Obbard

ISBN 0 904287 52 1

A catalogue record for this book is available
from the British Library

Set by Phoenix Typesetting, Ilkley, West Yorkshire

Printed and bound by The Cromwell Press, Broughton Gifford,
Wiltshire

Contents

Acknowledgements

My special thanks to Josef Pichler for permission to use his translation of the *Revelations of Divine Love* (abbreviated in the references to *RDL*).
To Sr. Christine Jasinski for typing the manuscript.
To my community for the time needed for writing.

And to all who have helped me to understand more deeply the meaning of God's love through sharing with me their own human love.

Introduction

This little work is intended to introduce Julian of Norwich to a wider readership by setting her in her own time and place and giving a selection of illustrated readings from her book *Revelations of Divine Love*.

As I have read and reread Julian over the years I have found in her a source of deep wisdom. Here is a woman who knew what it meant to wrestle with life's problems and questions. She did not live in an easy period of history yet she never lapsed into despair, denigration of others or a fatalistic attitude.

Julian is a woman of joy, of inner peace, of gratitude. She is also a woman with the courage to explore reality. Julian encourages us to keep on praying, to keep on trusting – in God and others – knowing that life is not absurd but has a divine purpose. Writing from the solitude of her anchorhold she is a symbol of the world's 'little people', those who feel themselves to be under-achievers, shackled to routine, people without power and without voice in the political arena. Julian, herself a 'nobody' by ordinary standards, discovered that her life, routine like that of hundreds of others in the big city, was mysteriously linked to *all* life; that her sorrows and joys were a microcosm of the whole of humanity.

Julian knew she was embedded in the very heart of creation, with God. Therefore nothing human was alien to her any more than it was to the Son of God who shared our flesh and blood and entered into human history as one of us.

Julian, a woman of her time, is equally a woman of ours, because she is a woman belonging unreservedly to Christ, 'the same yesterday, today and forever'. Therefore she can speak powerfully to each one who reads her book and ponders her insights. May she do so even now – to you.

1

Norfolk – Then and Now

Norfolk is a county dominated by sky. It arches over the flat land, giving one a sense of vastness and freedom. Daily the sun, which rises as a pale yellow globe from the direction of the sea, dispels the pre-dawn mist lying like a deep layer of cobweb over the fields. The horizon then quickly turns to white and the whole area above becomes delicate violet and then a deep, deep blue. On rainy days, of which there are many, the aerial expanse turns into a mass of cumulus clouds, grey and heaving, as if the sea had arisen from its bed to tower over the country in a canopy of wetness. Then with the approach of evening the same sun – round, round as a huge red hazelnut in a pool of orange and purple light – bows to the blackness of night. Yes, Norfolk is sky even before one thinks of the land beneath it, though that too has its beauty.

Compared with industrial England, East Anglia is still unspoiled, agricultural, with blossoming fields of lavender and yellow rape-seed stretching for acres across the flat plains. Fields of wheat are clotted with poppies in summer; then when autumn arrives pyramids of murky bronze sugar beet await collection. Sheep, many of them the hardy, horned Norfolk breed with black quizzical faces, stay out of doors most of the year, moving from field to field as they crop them to near baldness.

The wide, open landscape leaves parish churches visible for miles: beautiful churches with fine carvings and painted rood screens (if they escaped the destruction of the Reformers). There are more churches in Norfolk than in any other county of comparable size and often seven or more towers can be seen from a single point.

In Norfolk pheasants make free with the roads, ignoring passing cars until the last moment, when they rise, squawking throatily, to disappear into the clouds of Queen Anne's lace decorating the grass verge. Seagulls fly well inland, following the plough, avid for worms in the new-turned loam. As they fly, the sun catches their wings – white, white in the expanse of blue.

No wonder that Norfolk people feel bound to the sky and land that has borne them. Here it is easy to put down roots and thrive; while those who have spent a lifetime in these hamlets and passed from infancy to adulthood beneath the spire of their parish church term themselves 'genuine Norfolk dumplings' with all the pride of a St Paul boasting of his ancestry as 'a true Israelite of the tribe of Benjamin'.

Norfolk is a way of life. Land and sky enter the bloodstream and change one's perceptions . . . Norfolk! It is a county which encourages pondering, a county which in medieval times was a busy thoroughfare, thick with monastic foundations, pilgrims and people of all kinds, an area of almost unparallelled prosperity.

In the Middle Ages not only was Norfolk intensively farmed but it was *the* wool manufacturing county of all England, famous for its worsted cloth. The money from the wool trade built these magnificent churches, some almost cathedral-like in their size and beauty, and decorated by the best craftsmen, providing employment for the skilled artisan in a way that many today would envy – even the meanest carpenter, stonemason or painter had an outlet for his creativity.

North Norfolk boasted a shrine of international importance at Walsingham, attracting pilgrims from the Continent who disembarked at Lynn or Wells and made their way overland to the great Augustinian Priory. The Kings of England patronized this shrine, travelling in state with their gentlemen at arms, valets, cooks and full royal retinue. Crowds of humbler folk, the sick, the poor, the limbless, the deformed, the mute, the insane were seen converging on the village. They had come to pray in the little wooden house of the Annunciation enclosed in the magnificent Priory Church. This Shrine owed its beginnings to Richeldis de Faverches, lady of the manor of Walsingham probably around the beginning of the twelfth century. She had erected a wooden chapel built after the pattern of Mary's house at Nazareth and there the mystery of the Annunciation, 'Gabriel's Ave', found a focus. The popularity of Richeldis's chapel grew swiftly, causing it to be duly housed in a stone church and cared for by Canons of St Augustine. Soon it contained a much venerated and bejewelled image of Our Lady with the child on her knee, and beneath her feet a green toadstone, an East Anglian symbol of evil.

Pilgrims thronged Norfolk-wards, bringing trade to hospices, innkeepers, merchants, village farmers and souvenir manufacturers (for all pilgrims would want to purchase a badge to show they had reached their destination safely). Those who slept rough and watched the stars of the Milky Way glittering in the black basin of night called it the Walsingham Way in homage to Mary.

The Pynson Ballad, written around 1465, many years after Walsingham had become famous, gives us an idea of the Shrine's origins and the thousands who travelled there seeking healing. Walsingham was not the only place of pilgrimage in Norfolk but it was by far the most important. It earned the village the title of England's holy land as the ballad says, and *all* England, because of it, was called Mary's Dowry.

O England, you have every reason
to be happily compared to the Promised
                    Land of Sion.
This glorious lady's grace and support
enable you to be called everywhere the
            holy land, our Lady's Dowry
as you have been named from the beginning.

The likely cause of this title
is that here is built this house in new
                            Nazareth,

to the honour of the Queen of heaven and
                                                          her glorious salutation.
'Ave', Gabriel's greeting at old Nazareth,
is daily remembered here as your joy.

O gracious Lady, glory of Jerusalem,
cypress of Sion, joy of Israel,
Rose of Jericho, Star of Bethlehem,
do not despise our petitions.
You are blessed above all women,
therefore grant your bounteous grace to all
                        who devoutly visit you here.

In the middle of the county its chief town, Norwich,
was second in importance only to London. Built on a
bend of the River Wensum, which joins the Yare and
gives access to the sea at Yarmouth, medieval Norwich
was, as it is today, a city of distinction.

Its focal point was the Cathedral of the Holy Trinity,
erected by Norwich's first bishop, Herbert de Losinga,
who transferred the episcopal see there from Thetford.
An abbey for sixty Benedictine monks was attached to
the cathedral to ensure a reverent celebration of the daily
offices. Then there were numerous parish churches
within the city walls as well as guild chapels and an
anchorhold at every city gate.

Norwich was the centre of the wool manufacturing trade and hence attracted numerous merchants,
especially from Flanders. With the Hundred Years War
in progress many ports on the South Coast were

considered dangerous because of their proximity to France. But Norfolk, bulging into the sea further up England, was safe for trade export and import; and Norwich, accessible by river yet well away from any possible coastal attack, throve and prospered. The city and its markets were the throbbing pulse of the county. Lords, merchants, artisans, peasants jostled together in the city streets. The ever-present animals – pigs, goats, dogs, rats – snuffled in the trenches of slops and offal that ran down the middle of the roads. Dyers, weavers, parchment makers, tailors, haggled over sheepskins. Peasants brought fruit and vegetables from the outlying villages. Monks, friars, priests could be seen in the general mêlée (nuns were supposed to stay inside their convents!). The languages heard were as cosmopolitan as the people. English was the tongue of the 'common herd', French the language of society, Latin that of the Church. From groups of merchants might float the guttural German of the Rhineland, the flat Flemish of travelling traders, or the excited tones of Italian painters.

Norwich too had its own centre of pilgrimage, the shrine of 'Little St William', a young boy reputedly murdered by Jews and whose tomb was in the cathedral. There seems to be no basis whatever for the legend that was similar to that of 'Little St Hugh' as told by the Prioress in the *Canterbury Tales*, except that William's body had been found in a wood and *someone* had to take the blame! So pilgrims – to Norwich and en route to Walsingham – added to the city crowds.

Religious and secular life were intertwined so closely

no one even tried to separate them. The liturgical year with its fasts and feasts, the guilds with their mystery plays, the celebration of the sacraments at each important rite of passage – these were taken for granted – just as was the necessity to draw water daily from well or river, the struggle to make a fortune (or at least a comfortable living), the need to eat and sleep and make love. And over all, the ever-present possibility of sickness and death, with which everyone lived in close proximity. No wonder the crucified Christ was constantly before people's eyes. Someone had suffered and struggled as one of themselves before attaining the final victory.

2

Julian – Woman of Norwich

In this city of Norwich in 1342, just as autumn had turned the trees leafless and the wind blew over the flat land from the sea, chilling bones and houses in its unimpeded course, a child was born in one of these crowded streets – a girl child who was to have an almost unparalleled influence on today's religious thought. But at the time of her birth she was so unregarded we know neither her parentage nor her baptismal name, so we can only call her by her later 'adopted' name – Julian.

It was the reign of Edward III, a time of increasing poverty and social unrest. The Hundred Years War was still in progress, taking men away to fight and draining the populace of resources through the levelling of high taxes.

The child Julian would have spent her early years swaddled tightly in bands, suckled either by mother or nursemaid depending on her social status, and being inserted into the life of the city. There would be places to visit, friends to make, games to play as with children everywhere.

Then tragedy entered her young life. When Julian was six years old the bubonic plague arrived in Norwich, travelling across England from Dorset carried by fleas which bred in the hairs of the black rat. The child would have known the sudden shattering of her secure world. With the dreaded Black Death men and women could rise in the morning feeling healthy and be dead by evening, their faces bloated, their bodies already near decomposition. The plague struck wealthy and humble indiscriminately. Priests who tried to minister to the dying quickly succumbed themselves. Religious houses were depleted. Terror reigned. At night the death carts rattled through the alleys, and houses would yield up their dead if any of their inhabitants were well enough to drag out the corpses within. Great pits received the bodies; thousands died unshriven, and relatives mourned not only the loss but the possible eternal damnation of their loved ones.

By the time Julian was seven the plague had moved on, but it had left scarcely any family complete. Death, ever-present even at the best of times in medieval England, had made its indelible mark on the child.

However, life soon returns to normal, such is human resilience. Merchants once more took up business, weavers and dyers their looms and vats, hostels re-opened. But Julian's childhood would have been short as well as sombre. A little girl must learn early to be of help to her mother in domestic tasks and know how to govern her own household when barely past puberty. There would be visits to the market where herrings, responsible for the prosperity of Yarmouth, were shipped down the Yare and Wensum to find their place as a staple food, laid on slabs at the docks, great barrels of them being opened to display glinting round scales of red-bronze. There would be the need to buy and preserve food, to weave, to sew, to cook or supervise cooking, to gather firewood, draw water, make tallow dips, and bond with other girls as they discussed future husbands – husbands almost certainly chosen by parents and with whom they could hope, despite their fears, for a relationship of mutual love and equal partnership. Then in the long, dark evenings the family would gather round the fire in the middle of the room, a fire burning in clay pit or brazier (as fire bricks were still not invented), and there sew near-sightedly in the dim glow or sit listening to stories and songs before an early bed in a smoke-filled side-chamber.

A girl could expect to be married at around fifteen, unless she entered a convent at approximately the same age. As Julian makes no reference to convent living or nuns in her writings, we may assume she followed the general custom, and thus wedlock and childbearing marked her passage from maidenhood to wife and mother. Then in 1361 the plague returned to Norwich, this time in a form particularly virulent to children. Julian was nineteen. The same sights, sounds, smells of childhood were revived and possibly by the end of that year Julian was without husband or child. But Norwich, like the phoenix later carved on its magnificent cathedral pulpit, rose from the ashes of death once more. A veritable reassertion of life began in the rebuilding and redecorating of many of its churches, and even when the cathedral spire was blown down in a great gale in 1362 the people only redoubled their efforts to prove their resilience and 'choose life'.

Meanwhile, we may look briefly at Julian's religious awakening and development. She would have been inserted early into a Christianity that pervaded city life – the ceremonies of cathedral and churches, monks singing the offices, friars preaching and being closely involved in social concerns. There was a Benedictine convent for women at Carrow where Julian might possibly have received a rudimentary education if her family were sufficiently wealthy. But this is doubtful, simply because, as said before, she shows no interest in or knowledge of such a life. God for her is a 'homely' lover rather than a *personal* 'Bridegroom'.

Julian was a deeply religious young laywoman, touched early by death and sorrow. She had seen people die without the sacraments and had known suffering in her own life. Like many before and since she had turned to the Crucified, and, as she tells us herself, had begged God for three gifts.

The first was recollection of the Passion. The second was a physical sickness at the young age of thirty. The third was to receive three wounds as God's gift.

As far as the first goes, I thought I had already experienced something of the Passion of Christ; yet, by the grace of God, I desired still more. I wished I had really been there with Mary Magdalene and the others who loved him, in order to see with my own eyes the Passion that Our Lord suffered for me, and so be able to suffer with him, as was granted to those who loved him and were near to him. For this reason I wanted to have a bodily vision through which I could understand better the physical pains of Our Lord and the compassion of Our Lady and of all his true lovers alive at the time who saw his pains. I wanted to have been one of them and have suffered with them. Apart from this I never had any other desire for a vision or revelation from God, until my soul would depart from the body (for I believed that I would be saved by the mercy of God). The reason for this prayer was that after the vision I might more truly understand the Passion of Christ.

With regard to the second gift, it came to my mind with a condition, freely and without my seeking it. It was an intense desire to have from God the gift of a physical illness. I wanted this illness to be severe even to the point of death so that I could receive all the rites of Holy Church, I myself being convinced that I would die, and that also all the others that saw me should think the same. I did not want to have any kind of comfort that earthly life can offer. I wanted to have all the different pains, physical and spiritual, that I would have had had I really died, with all the fears and temptations of the devils, and every other kind of pain except the actual departure of the soul. I desired this because I wanted to be fully cleansed by the mercy of God, and afterwards, as a result of this sickness, live a more consecrated life for the glory of God. I hoped that this would be to my advantage after my death, for I desired soon to be with my God and Maker.

These two desires, for the Passion and the sickness, I asked God for conditionally, because it seemed to me that this was not the ordinary practice of prayer. Therefore I said: 'Lord, you know what I want, if it is your will let me have it . . . but if it is not your will, good Lord, do not be angry, for I want nothing that is not your will.'

As for the third gift, by the grace of God and the teaching of Holy Church, I developed a strong desire to receive three wounds during my life; that is to say, the wound of true contrition, the wound of natural compassion, and the wound of unshakable longing for God. And as I prayed for the other two gifts unconditionally, so I prayed for this third one without condition. The first two desires I soon forgot, but the third remained with me continually. (*RDL* ch.2)

We could note here that Julian was already devoted to meditating on Christ's passion, a common focus of devotion when life was harsh and the Man of Sorrows was seen as 'one of the people', helpless and poor. But Julian wanted to experience this in a deeper, more personal and visual way so as to empathize with him more, really 'feel' for and with him as if she had been present on Calvary. Then she wanted to receive the last sacraments (given only at the point of death in those days), thus she would have to know the extremes of bodily sickness. Anointing and shriving she hoped would dispose her for a more serious and dedicated Christian life. Lastly she wanted three wounds, wounds of contrition, compassion and longing for God. As a stimulus towards this she tells us elsewhere (in the Shorter Version of her

Shewings) that this request was inspired by a sermon on St Cecilia who was reputed to have received three sword thrusts in the neck before dying. Here Julian's originality is already apparent. She does not want wounds of martyrdom, nor even the wounds of Christ (the stigmata so greatly desired by many women mystics on the Continent). Instead she asks for three interior wounds that she herself chooses: the wound of sorrow for sin; the wound of 'natural compassion' for Christ's suffering (that is, to think of *him* and not wallow in self or in personal sorrow); the wound of longing for God (since we become what we desire).

The first two gifts which Julian had prayed for in a moment of youthful fervour were forgotten as life took its daily course; they surfaced only later from the subconscious when the Lord took her at her word. But the third gift, that of the three wounds, she never forgot. These were the focus of her daily spiritual growth and needed no special divine intervention. They are gifts *all* Christians might profit from; and Julian felt absolutely 'at one' with all her fellow-Christians ('even-Christians' she calls them in the language of her day) of whom she was to become a living symbol and embodiment.

3

8th May 1373

Life continued. Julian worked and prayed, went to market, managed her household, talked with her friends, listened to sermons, involved herself in social life. She was now thirty and a half, early middle age when life expectancy was fifty if one was fortunate. But as her mother was still alive Julian could well have considered herself relatively youthful.

It was Eastertide. She had attended all the services of the Passion, kissing the elevated Cross on Good Friday, visiting the sepulchre on the Saturday of Holy Week, rejoicing in the candlelit church as the Resurrection was celebrated on Easter Sunday. It would be a time of renewed personal dedication, the season for her annual confession and communion in an age when the laity received the sacrament once a year and even professed monks and nuns communicated very infrequently. Doubtless it was also a time when she meditated more deeply on the three wounds she constantly desired.

But as the Paschal season continued and spring moved across the city with its promise of new life in the soft pink arch of the sky, the flowers nosing through the grass and tree buds swelling and bursting, Julian faced death. It was early May. For three days and nights she lay prostrated by her illness, and on the fourth day she received the last sacraments. But she was tenacious of life. She wanted to *live*. She lingered on for two more days and nights. By the third night she and those who were with her were certain death was imminent.

> As I was still young I thought it was extremely sad to die, not that there was anything on earth I wanted to live for, nor was I sad because I was afraid of the pain, for I totally trusted in God's mercy. But the reason I wanted to live was so that I could love God better, and for a longer time, and by virtue of this living know God better and love him more deeply in the bliss of heaven. For it seemed to me that all my life here on earth had been very paltry and short compared to eternal bliss. I thought: 'Good Lord, may I no longer live to your glory?' But my reason and the pain that I was enduring suggested to me that I would die. And I assented fully with all the will of my heart to the will of God. (*RDL* ch.3:2)

The next day the priest was sent for so that he could be present at her passing. He came bringing a crucifix and attended by a young boy. Already Julian was paralysed from the waist down and had to be supported when she tried to sit upright and prepare herself for the end. The paralysis slowly spread through all her limbs. She was helpless.

Gazing at the crucifix the priest had brought to comfort her in her agony she saw the figure on the cross emanating light and inculcating peace, and just as she thought her last moment had come she suddenly felt well and whole. Then she remembered her former desires. She had already received the first gift of illness to the point of death, now she asked for the second one, the gift of experiencing the Passion of Christ as though actually present. And as she asked she entered into a visionary state where the crucifix became living and real.

And immediately I saw the red blood trickle down from under the garland of thorns, a living stream of hot, fresh blood, just as it was at the time of his Passion when the crown of thorns was pressed on his blessed head. And I saw very clearly and powerfully that he, both God and man, who suffered for me, was the very same one who showed this vision to me without any go-between.

And in the same vision, the Trinity suddenly filled my heart with the deepest joy. I immediately realised that this will be the permanent experience of those who go to heaven. For the Trinity is God. God is the Trinity. The Trinity is our maker, the Trinity is our keeper, the Trinity is our everlasting lover, the Trinity is our endless joy and bliss, through our Lord Jesus Christ and in our Lord Jesus Christ. And this was shown to me in the first revelation and in all the others, for wherever Jesus appears, the whole blessed Trinity is to be understood, as I see it. And I said: '*Benedicite Domine!*' This I said out of reverence in a powerful voice, and I was absolutely overwhelmed with wonder and marvel to see that he who is so holy and so awesome, should be so homely with a sinful creature living in this wretched flesh.

I understood this vision to be a time of grace, in which our Lord Jesus, out of his tender love, wanted to give me some comfort before I would be tempted. For it seemed to me that with the permission of God and under his protection I might well be tempted by devils before I died. But I knew well that with this vision of his blessed Passion, along with the Godhead that I saw in my understanding, there was enough strength to enable me, and indeed all living creatures who will be saved, to withstand all the devils of hell and every spiritual temptation. (*RDL* ch.4:1–3)

At the beginning of her *Shewings* Julian was still convinced she would die of her illness and that she was being strengthened to meet the final judgement. Her mother thought so too, and had even leant over her to close the glazed eyes. But Julian did not die. Her visions continued for a day and a night and part of the next day, covering many themes simultaneously which Julian apprehended with a sense of diffuse awareness.

During those sixteen *Shewings* she learnt much that had yet to be brought into focused consciousness, ruminated on and finally committed to writing. She was sure she had seen important things, not because she was worthy, but because as a Christian, united with other Christians in the Church, she had been granted an insight that was intended to be shared.

Everything that I am saying about myself I mean to say about all my fellow-Christians, for I was taught in the spiritual vision that this is what Our Lord God intends it for. Therefore I beg you all for God's sake, and I advise you for your own benefit, that you stop thinking about the poor wretch to whom the vision was shown, but that you better, powerfully, wisely and humbly contemplate God himself, who in his courteous love and in his endless goodness wanted to show these things to all, so that all might be comforted. It is God's will that you accept it with the greatest joy and delight, as if Jesus himself had shown it to *you*.

I am not good because of this vision, but only if I love God more because of it. And to the extent that you love God more than I do, you are that much better than I am. I am not saying this to those who are wise, for they know it well enough. But I am saying it to you who are simple, to give you peace and comfort, for we are in fact all one in love. And truly it was not shown to me that God loves me more than the least soul that is in the state of grace. I am sure that there are many who never had any revelations or visions outside the ordinary teaching of Holy Church and yet who love God more than I do. If I look at myself alone, I am nothing at all, but in the whole body of Christ, I am, I hope, united in love with all my fellow-Christians. (*RDL* ch.8:6; ch.9:1)

Julian had seen and experienced much in a very short time, and as far as we know she never had any further revelation or vision in her long life (unlike many Continental mystics whose visions were continuous or stretched over long periods of time). Within two days she had apprehended something of the mystery of Christ's Passion, the Trinity, and Mary mother of the Lord. She had experienced deep emotions of joy, sorrow, tenderness, compassion, wonder. She had learned lessons on prayer, on the goodness of creation yet its insignificance in comparison to God. She had experienced the homeliness and intimacy of God's love; learned lessons about sin, salvation and grace; apprehended the reality of our union with one another and the links that bind people together.

What then was she to do? She recovered her health; but a return to 'normal' life would give little leisure for pondering and sifting her new-found insights. She had no desire to be a nun who would lead an almost equally busy life within her convent as well as following a strictly regulated timetable.

It seems that some time after her *Shewings* Julian retired to an anchorhold beside the Church of St Julian and St Edward at Conisford, Norwich, and there she devoted the rest of her life to pondering over what she had seen and heard in those packed hours when death was close. What she wrote was first recorded in a document entitled *A Shewing of God's Love*, giving a brief account of her visions and the circumstances in which she received them. Then about twenty years later, after much prayer and solitary reflection, she composed a longer version, containing expanded teaching on various themes. The earlier book was a tiny seed, the later one displayed the ripe fruit of her spiritual maturity. She would then have been fifty years old and was to live on for at least another twenty-three years, as she is last mentioned in a will in 1416. It was a fine old age for one who had thought, when her visions began, that she was about to die at the age of thirty!

Julian in her anchorhold was revered as a wise counsellor and a woman of God, but her young life passed into oblivion. Who she was, whereabouts in the city she had lived, who were her family and forebears – all this was forgotten. She became just 'the lady at St Julian's', contracted speedily and informally to 'the lady Julian' – and by this name only do we now know her.

4

Life in St Julian's Anchorhold

Whether Julian was enclosed in an already existing anchorhold that had fallen vacant or whether she had one specially built for herself we do not know. There were already a number of solitaries in the city, and one more would arouse no special comment. It was a time in England when this vocation was held in high regard. All the English mystical writers contemporary with Julian were associated in some way with the solitary life. Richard Rolle, who died of the plague in Hampole when Julian was seven, had spent most of his adult years as a wandering hermit and wrote lyrically of its joys. Walter Hilton who died in 1395 had written his *Ladder of Perfection* for an anchoress, and the anonymous author of *The Cloud of Unknowing* wrote for a young intending hermit. The thirteenth-century *Ancrene Riwle*, which gives us much knowledge of the practical aspects of this life, was written for three recluses around the Salisbury area. The fourteenth century saw the growth and popularity of the Carthusian Order in England which, amid the general decline of standards precipitated by the Black

Death, kept its ideals high and its selection of candidates rigorous.

The solitary life could be embraced either by professed religious – monks and nuns of an order – or by lay people, though evidence suggests that lay people predominated. Most monasteries and convents were loath to lose a valuable subject, though a later Julian in Norwich who became an anchoress, Dame Julian Lampyt, was probably a nun of Carrow Priory. Men who became hermits could, if they wished, live in the countryside, perhaps serving the populace by keeping roads and bridges in good repair and offering hospitality to the occasional wayfarer. Women on the other hand had to stay near inhabited places for safety, where their material needs could be suitably supplied, and several women might even live together (as envisioned in the *Ancrene Riwle*). An anchorhold could consist of a single room or several rooms (like a small bungalow); some women owned a piece of enclosed garden where vegetables and flowers could be grown and the solitary breathe fresh air beneath the open sky. A servant was needed to bring water, empty slops, cook food and run errands. Julian, as we learn from wills, had at some point a servant named Sara and another named Alice. *The Ancrene Riwle* allows for two servants and regulates in detail for their conduct outside the anchorhold, with each other and with their mistress.

While the rule of enclosure was strictly adhered to – an anchoress could not go outside her designated domain – life within it was relatively balanced and humane. Food was to be nourishing and well served, clothes warm but simple in design. Cleanliness was encouraged and all harsh penances eschewed. This was not the life of a desert father but of a tempered asceticism. Prayers were recited at set times during the day; psalms and other devotions – to the wounds of Christ, to Mary his mother, to the Blessed Sacrament – were prescribed, but books would be few. These were precious and for the most part securely secreted in monastic libraries. An anchoress, while not allowed to go out, seems exceptionally to have been allowed visitors inside. Presumably her servant would have access if the anchoress was ill, or perhaps an important benefactor or someone seeking extended counsel could enter likewise. But it must be a woman; no man might come in or even spend long in conversation at her window-on-the-world. As the *Ancrene Riwle* forbids its solitaries to teach children, it may have been customary for some children to be admitted for instruction on the rudiments of the ABC. This would be one way for a lone woman to earn her keep – for servants must be paid, material needs provided for, and while alms might be plentiful it was considered good to be occupied with sewing, embroidery or other handwork to supplement one's income and avoid idleness.

An anchorhold had three windows, one looking on to the sanctuary of the adjoining Church, one on to the road (to which people could come for counsel) and one to admit light. There may have been others, but in the custom of the time all would have been small as heat must be conserved, and the window-on-the-world had to be covered with a thick black cloth embroidered with a white cross.

The hours of daylight would be spent reciting the pre-scribed vocal prayers, 'attending' Mass kneeling by the sanctuary window, and giving counsel to those who came by. But there were too the long winter nights, when darkness came early and a few rushes from the floor might glow dimly for a few moments when dipped in oil. Plenty of opportunity then to ponder and pray; for in the silent darkness people did not venture out in the unlit streets looking for an anchoress's prayers or advice.

A woman who had convinced the Bishop of her suit-ability for the solitary life was officially enclosed in her anchorhold at the end of a solemn ceremony. Often a Mass of the Dead was celebrated, the aspirant voiced her intention to live as a recluse and received her plain tunic and veil to show she had renounced 'the world and every adornment for love of our Lord Jesus Christ'. Sometimes the antiphon '*O clavis David*' was intoned from the Advent Liturgy as the anchoress entered her enclosure:

O key of David and sceptre of Israel,
what you open no one can close again;
what you close no one can open.
O come to lead the captive from prison;
free those who sit in darkness and in
                              the shadow of death.

It was a prayer that, while God enclosed the recluse in what looked like a prison, he would open wide the door to liberty of spirit, that she might walk in God's kingdom where no doors could be shut against her.

We have no details of the anchorhold beside St Julian's, Conisford. I imagine it as being one room with a curtained-off area of rough hangings behind which would be a bed and a privy. The living space consisted of table, stool, devotional corner, a chest for clothes and other possessions, and the three windows, one on to the sanctuary, one on to the road, and one on to a small patch of enclosed garden. A communicating door led into the servants' room with a hatch above, at which messages could be given.

Life for a recluse was not all prayers, handwork and being a ready listener for those in need. It would be wrong not to stress the time it must have taken in those days just to *live* – dependent on a servant for daily food and water – water that had to be supplied for all personal washing and cleaning. Then one's room had to be kept in order, one's person tidy and dignified without lapsing into over-fastidiousness or slovenliness. Julian's long life argues a cleanliness and an inner and outer balance which are reflected in her book. Her images are homely and she shows great reverence towards all bodily functions – for example:

A man goes upright, and the food that he eats is preserved in his body as in a most beautiful purse. When it is necessary, the purse opens and then it is shut again in full honesty. And that it is God who does this is shown there where he says that he comes down to the lowest part of our need. For he does not despise what he has made, nor does he disdain to serve us even in the simplest of our natural bodily functions, for he loves the soul that he has made in his own likeness. For just as the body is clad in clothes, and the flesh in skin, and the bones in the flesh, and the heart in the whole, so are we, body and soul, clad and enclosed in the goodness of God. Yes, and even more intimately because all these other things may wear out and vanish, but the goodness of God is always whole and close to us without compare. (*RDL* ch.6:5)

Then Julian might have had a small garden to tend, be expected to show concern for her servant's welfare and be available for mending clothes and other acts of charity. As a cat was permitted by the *Ancrene Riwle* I feel sure Julian would have had one, not just to keep rodents at bay but to provide a little company.

During Julian's time within her enclosure city life continued to swirl around her. She would hear of the pressing social and religious concerns that shook East Anglia in the wake of the changing social conditions that followed on the Black Death. In June 1381 the Peasants' Revolt, which had begun with the Essex priest John Ball, reached Norwich. It symbolized the accumulated grievances of the poor, tied to a land they could not own, depleted and impoverished by disease, taxed by levies to finance a war they had no interest in save to see it stopped. Marchers entered Norwich and were brutally handled by the Bishop, Henry Despenser. Julian would have heard of the public, bloody executions. An unorganized uprising thus ended in carnage and bloodshed, and as usual many innocent people suffered, among them the poorest and most downtrodden.

The Lollards, followers of Wyclif, were also tried and harried to their deaths as heretics if found within the city walls. The smell of their burning in the 'Lollard pits' close by would have wafted over the air into Julian's cell, filling her with foreboding. She could not equate God's mercy and love with eternal damnation for Jews and heretics as taught by the Church of her time. Her own attitude to 'outsiders' was mild and humble, which speaks much for a woman whose city Cathedral housed the pilgrimage shrine of 'Little St William'.

One of Julian's visitors we do know. Marjorie Kemp was wife of one of Lynn's leading citizens and as different from Julian as one woman could be from another. Having borne fourteen children she had persuaded her husband to live with her in continence (a rather one-sided inspiration one gathers). She spent her time going on pilgrimages as far afield as the Holy Land and Italy, where her loud sobbing caused annoyance to fellow travellers and those trying to pray in less conspicuous ways. Marjorie was the first English person to write an autobiography (another 'first' for Norfolk!) but her eccentric piety forced her to seek reassurance from all quarters and she came to Norwich to consult three people about her spiritual state: Richard de Caister (a priest), the Carmelite William Sowthfeld, and the anchoress 'Dame

Jelyan'. Richard de Caister, renowned for his holiness, was revered as a saint for a while after his death. Marjorie's book gives us our only evidence for the impact of William and Julian on contemporary life. Marjorie's visit to Julian, fully recounted, shows her as a wise and prudent counsellor, and she gave her strange visitor several days of attention, far more than either of the men! Marjorie was extremely grateful – but not so reassured that she stopped consulting others.

Meanwhile, during her years of reclusion, Julian was finding time to write or dictate her *Shewings* and the meaning she was discovering in them. She terms herself 'unlettered' and most likely she was. There was little if any schooling available for women; most could neither read nor write and even nuns recited the office by rote learning. Either Julian taught herself to read and write in order to communicate her insights, or she dictated to a scribe. The former seems more likely as the finished book has many cross-references; and also long periods spent with a scribe would be frowned upon as giving cause for scandal. So Julian wrote – wrote for the first time a spiritual treatise in the language of the common people – not French, not Latin, but in a tongue still newly born, with its peculiar richness and rhythm. Julian 'the unlettered' produced a masterpiece. There is nothing to compare it with for it is unique. Julian is the acknowledged 'first lady' of written English.

5

Julian – Writer and Theologian

Julian had seen wondrous things that memorable 8th May, but what did they all *mean*? Was there some theme tune that could be picked out from the varied harmony and counterpoint of the music? At the end of long, hard reflection she concluded her book thus:

From the time I first had these revelations I often longed to know what our Lord meant. More than fifteen years later I was given in response a spiritual understanding and I was told: 'Do you want to know what our Lord meant in all this? Know it well: Love was his meaning. Who showed it to you? Love. What did he show you? Love. Why did he show it to you? For Love. Remain firm in this love, and you will taste of it ever more deeply, but you will never know anything else from it for ever and ever.'

So I was taught that love was what our Lord meant. And I saw with absolute certainty in this revelation and in all the rest that before God made us he loved us and that this love never slackened, nor ever will. In this love he has done all his works, in this love he has made all things for our benefit, and in this love our life is everlasting. In our creation we had a beginning, but the love in which he created us was in him for ever and without beginning. In this love we have our beginning. And all this we shall see in God without end. (*RDL* ch.86:3,4)

Love was the unifying theme – tender, dependable, utterly trustworthy love.

But if love is the leitmotif of the *Revelations*, where does sin come in? Julian is no naïve woman, unaware of the power of sin in herself, in others and in the world at large. However, while acknowledging that sin is a mystery, she refuses to respond to it by activating the motive of fear. Julian countenances no theories that show God as on the watch, waiting to condemn and punish the weak and the sinful. Instead, she sets sin within the wider context of a creator who cherishes rather than condemns. Sin is only *part* of a whole in which grace and forgiveness predominate.

At this point I paused to contemplate the whole thing in general, darkly and mournfully, saying mentally to our Lord with great fear: 'Ah, good Lord, how can all be well in view of the great harm sin has brought to your creatures?' And with this I desired (as much as I dared) to have a fuller explanation by which my mind would be put at ease regarding this matter. To this our blessed Lord answered very gently and with a most loving expression, showing me that the sin of Adam was the greatest harm that had ever been done or ever will be done until the end of the world. And he also showed me that this is clearly known to Holy Church on earth. Furthermore, he told me to contemplate the glorious reparation he has made; for this reparation is far more pleasing to the blessed Godhead, and incomparably more valuable for our salvation, than the sin of Adam was harmful. This then is our blessed Lord's thinking: and his teaching is that we should pay special attention to this:

'Since I have made well the greatest harm, it is my will that you know from this that I shall make well all that is less harmful.' (*RDL* ch. 29)

Sin cannot ultimately have the last word, no matter how much suffering there is in the world, because Christ has conquered sin once and for all.

Julian is supremely orthodox in her thinking in that she does not see God and Satan as equals battling for human souls – a Good power versus an equally strong Evil power. No, the devil is in no way comparable to God; biblically the battle is between Lucifer and the Archangel Michael – this puts things in an entirely different perspective!

As for personal sin, we must avoid it from motives of love, not fear.

The same true love that touches us all with his blessed comfort, the very same blessed love teaches us to hate sin for love's sake alone. And I am certain from my own experience that the more each loving soul sees this in the courteous love of our Lord God, the greater will be its reluctance to sin, and the more will it be ashamed. If we could see spread out before us all the pain there is in hell, in purgatory and on earth: death and everything else on the one hand and on the other hand sin, we should rather choose all the pain than the sin. Sin is so vile and so much to be hated that no pain which is not sin can be compared with it. I was shown no more cruel hell than sin, because a loving soul hates no pain except sin. When we direct our attention to love and humility, by the working of mercy and grace we are made all beautiful and clean. (*RDL* ch.40)

If after all this we continue to look at ourselves and sink into fear and depression on account of our personal failures, that is not humility (as we might think) but blindness and weakness.

Love makes power and wisdom very meek to us. For just as God in his courtesy forgets our sin after we have repented, so likewise he wishes us to forget our sin especially as far as our unreasonable depression and our doubtful fears are concerned. (*RDL* ch.73)

For Julian, as for St Paul, 'All things work together for good for those who love God' (Rom.8:28). As for those who do not love and do not even *want* to love, what happens to them is not revealed. It is God's own secret.

Other aspects of her work link Julian with the women mystics on the Continent: devotion to the Cross, the Trinity, the Virgin, the Eucharist, but she treats each aspect in a way completely her own. The threads with which she works weave, as it were, soft, warm swaddling bands rather than some magnificent bridal brocade. She is far from the erotic imagery that dominates the writings of a Mechtilde of Magdeburg or, to a lesser extent, an Angela of Foligno. Julian's focus is on all that is homely and humble. She is child rather than bride – she symbolises *all* who love Christ, *all* fellow-Christians who are children of the same parent. God is Mother and Father as well as Lover, loving us just because we belong to him and not because we have 'earned' anything. And Julian draws her imagery from daily life in a way that truly inserts her into her own time and place. We feel she is an integrated woman, nothing is alien or purely secular; all is drawn into the whole, all that is familiar mirrors the divine. The blood of Christ is described as brownish red and thick:

> The abundance was like the drops of water that fall off the eaves of a roof after a heavy shower of rain, falling so thickly that it is beyond human skill to count them. And as they spread out on the forehead they were as round as a herring's scales.
>
> These three images came to my mind at the time: pellets, because of the roundness of the drops of the blood when they first appeared; herring's scales, because of their roundness spreading on the forehead; raindrops falling from the eaves of the house, because there were too many to count. (*RDL* ch.7:3,4)

The relationship of the Lord with his children is homely and courteous, like that of a Lord who treats a servant with both respect and genuine affection.

> To help me understand this he showed me this clear example: the greatest honour a great king or a nobleman can bestow upon a poor servant is to treat him as a personal friend, especially if he does it sincerely and whole-heartedly both in public and in private. Then the servant will think, 'See, what greater honour and joy could this nobleman give me than to show me, who am so little, such wonderful homeliness. Truly, it gives me more joy and pleasure than if he were to give me great gifts, while remaining a stranger to me in his behaviour.' This visual example was shown so mightily it was as if the man's heart could be carried away and that he almost forgot himself for joy over this marvellous homeliness. That's how it stands with our Lord Jesus and us. It seems to me that there can surely be no greater joy than that the one who is highest and mightiest, noblest and most worthy, should also be the one who is most lowly, humble, homely and courteous. And surely and truly he will make this marvellous joy our own when we shall see him. It is our good Lord's will for us that we believe and trust, enjoy and delight, comfort and solace ourselves as best we can, with his grace and with his help, until the time that we see him in reality. (*RDL* ch.7:6,7)

Above all, there is the wonderful picture of God's motherly caring:

This fair and lovely word 'Mother' is so sweet and gentle in itself that it cannot truly be said of anyone or to anyone except of him and to him who is the true mother of life and of all things. The properties of motherhood are: natural love, wisdom and knowledge, and this is God. Though, it is true, our physical giving birth is but little, humble and simple compared to our spiritual birth. Yet it is still he who is at work when his creatures give birth. A kind, loving mother who knows and understands the needs of her child, guards it most tenderly as the nature and state of motherhood demand it. And always as the child grows in stature, she changes her method but not her love. And when it gets older she allows it to be chastised in order to break down its faults and to enable the child to accept values and graces. This, along with everything that is lovely and good, is our Lord's work in those who do it.

So, he is our mother in nature by means of the working of grace in the lower part, out of love for the higher part. And he wants us to know this for he wants us to fasten all our love on to him. (*RDL* ch.60:7; ch.59:5)

Another characteristic of Julian's writing is that during the sixteen *Shewings* she recounts there is no linear development. The same themes recur cyclically in a typically feminine way, as if bound to the recurring life rhythm of the seasons. As she says, all that followed was already contained in the first *Shewing*, but as each theme recurs throughout the book it is seen from a slightly different angle. Everything is interwoven and interlocking in the song of God's love, there is no logical order, one just surrenders to the whole symphony in its entirety.

Julian was not a scholar or trained theologian, but she was certainly full of native wit and sound common sense, quick to draw conclusions, humorous, blunt. She does not conceal her loud laughter on her supposed deathbed and she encourages her friends to laugh with her when she sees the devil routed! There is no pious 'front' behind which she hides. That is why we know so much of her spirit, so little of her biographical details. With her and her relationship with God there is nothing forced. The Lord is courteous, kindly, and will accept only a response that is free – and this at a time when it was usual to compel belief by threat of burning at the stake. And when we fail and sin we are not blamed or punished, for there is no anger or vengefulness in God. We cannot understand now why there is evil, sin and suffering, but we can know that in the end *all will be well.*

Obviously the thing to do is to read Julian's book in its entirety, but here I have chosen twenty passages from her writings which I consider cover the main themes of her *Revelations.* As Julian wrote in such a way as to offer a return to the same subject from another angle, to enlarge or elucidate, I have in some cases juxtaposed passages which, though occurring apart in the original work, can illuminate the theme touched upon. These passages I hope will give the reader a 'taste' of Julian's spirituality – her childlike trust, her grappling with deep problems and her simplicity before God's majesty and the Passion of his Son. The pictures are meant to appeal, not to children, but to the child within each one of us that Julian is so conversant with: that inner child who longs to be spontaneous, to love and be loved in all simplicity, and yet often hangs back through fear or surface sophistication. Julian in her writings has a talent for penetrating the facade people so often erect around themselves, and she encourages us to get behind it and connect with the child who responds naturally, simply and joyfully to a love freely offered.

Julian's teaching is for each one of us. She *knew* that. She stands for us all and she will teach us, gently and courteously, something of her vision of God.

God's Enfolding Love

At the same time as I had the bodily vision of the bleeding head, our Good Lord also gave me a spiritual vision of his homely loving. I saw that he is to us everything that is good and comfortable for our help. He is our clothing which for love enwraps us and enfolds us, embraces us and fully shelters us; and with his tender love he is so close to us that he can never leave us. So I saw in this vision that he is everything that is good, as far as I could understand.

God is as truly our mother as he is our father. He revealed this in all the revelations, but especially in these sweet words where he says: 'It is I'. That is to say,

'It is I – the power and the goodness of fatherhood.
It is I – the wisdom and kindness of motherhood.
It is I – the Trinity.
It is I – the unity.
It is I – the supreme goodness of every
          kind of thing.
It is I – who make you to love.

It is I – who make you to long.
It is I – the endless fulfilling of all true desires.'

For the soul is highest, noblest and worthiest when it is lowest, humblest and gentlest.

So our Lady is our mother, and in Christ we are all enclosed in her and born of her, because she, who is the mother of our Saviour, is the mother of all who are being saved by our Saviour. And our Saviour is our true mother, in whom we are continually being born and we shall never come out of him.

(RDL ch.5:1; ch.59:2; ch.57:5)

Creator, Lover, Keeper

He showed me a little thing, no bigger than a hazelnut (as it seemed to me), lying in the palm of my hand, and it was as round as a ball. I looked at it with the eye of my understanding and thought: 'What can this be?' And I was answered generally: 'It is all that is made!' I gazed with astonishment, wondering how it could survive because of its littleness. It seemed to me that it should presently fall into nothingness. And I was answered in my mind: 'It lasts and always will last because God loves it.' And so everything receives its being from the love of God.

In this little thing I saw three truths: the first is that God made it, the second is that God loves it, the third is that God keeps it. But what did I really see? In truth I saw the Creator, the Lover, and the Keeper. For until I am substantially united to him, I can never have perfect rest and true happiness. I mean to say, that I must be so oned to him that no created thing can come between my God and me.

This little thing, it seemed to me, could have fallen into nothingness because of its littleness. We need to be aware of the littleness of created things in order to avoid being attached to them, and so come to love and possess God who is uncreated. For this is the reason why we are not fully at ease in heart and soul. We seek rest in insignificant things which can offer us no rest, and we do not know our God who is all-powerful, totally wise and good. He alone is true rest. God wishes to be known by us and he delights when we rest in him, for all that is less than him is not enough for us. This is the reason why no soul can be at rest until it is emptied of all created things. When the soul voluntarily and for love lets go of all created things in order to possess him who is all, then it is able to receive spiritual rest.

Our good Lord also showed me that it gives him great pleasure when a helpless soul comes to him, openly, plainly and humbly. From this vision I understood that the soul naturally longs to do this through the touch of the Holy Spirit: 'God in your goodness give me yourself, for you are enough for me. I can ask nothing less if I am truly to live for your glory. If I were to ask less I would always remain in need. Only in you do I have everything.'

These words of God's goodness are very dear to the soul and most nearly touching the will of our Lord; for his goodness fills all his creatures and all his blessed works, and surpasses them without end. For he himself is the Eternal and he made us for himself alone, and restored us by his most precious Passion and is always keeping us safe in his blessed love. All this is the work of his goodness.

(RDL ch.5:2–7)

God Never Leaves Us

At one time my mind was led down to the bottom of the sea, and there I saw hills and green valleys seeming as if they were covered with moss, seaweed and gravel. Then I understood this to mean that, even if a man or a woman were under deep water, they would be safe in body and soul and come to no harm if they could see God who is with us all the time. And moreover, they would have more consolation and comfort than all this world can tell. For God wills that we believe that we see him all the time even though the seeing is very little. And in this faith he makes us grow ever more in grace, because he wants to be seen and he wants to be sought; he wants to be awaited and he wants to be trusted.

(*RDL* ch.10:3)

God Does All

After this I saw God in a point (that is to say in my mind),
by which vision I saw that he is in all things. I looked at
it carefully, seeing and recognizing through it that he
does all that is done. I marvelled at this vision with a
slight fear, and I thought: 'What is sin?' For I saw truly
that God does all things, however small they may be.
And I saw very clearly that nothing is done by chance or
luck, but all is done by the foreseeing wisdom of God. If
it seems like chance or luck in our eyes, the reason for
that is our blindness and lack of foresight. For those
things that are in God's foreseeing wisdom from all eter-
nity, and which he so rightly and to his glory continually
brings to their best conclusion, seem to fall on us out of
the blue, catching us unawares. So in our blindness and
lack of foresight we say: 'It is all luck and chance.' But to
our Lord it is not so.

This is what I understood in this revelation of love, for
I know well that in the eyes of our Lord God there is no
chance or luck. This compelled me to admit that everything that is done is well done, for God our Lord does all.

At this time I was not shown the working of God's creatures, but only the working of God *in* his creatures. He is at the centre of all, and he does everything. And I was certain that he does no sin. From this I understood that sin is not a deed, not a thing that is done, because in all this I was shown no sin. So I decided not to go on wondering and puzzling about this matter, but to look at the Lord and see what he would show me. And so, as far as I could take in at the time, the soul was shown the rightfulness of God's actions. Rightfulness has two fine qualities: it is right and it is full. And that is what all the works of our Lord are. Therefore they have no need of the work of mercy and grace, because they are totally right and they lack absolutely nothing.

This vision was shown to teach me that our Lord wants the soul to turn around and sincerely contemplate him and all his works. For they are totally good, and all his decrees are easy and sweet. They bring great peace to the soul that has turned away from contemplating the blind pronouncements of mortals to focus on the lovely and delightful decrees of our Lord God. A person may see some deeds as done well and others as evil, but our Lord does not see them like this. For just as all that exists in nature is the work of God so likewise do all deeds bear the stamp of God's doing. It is easy to understand that the best of deeds is done well; but the most insignificant deed that is being done is done just as well as the best and the greatest. Everything is according to the quality and in the order ordained by God even before the world began. For there is no doer but God.

I saw with absolute certainty that he never changes his purpose in anything, nor ever will without end. For there was nothing unknown to him in his rightful ordering of things from the very beginning. Therefore everything was set in order before anything was made so that it would endure for ever. And no manner of thing will fall short of this principle because he has made all things perfectly good.

And therefore the Blessed Trinity is always fully pleased with all its works. God revealed all this to me with great happiness as if to say: 'See, I am God. See, I am in all things. See, I do all things. See, I never lift my hands from my works, nor ever shall without end.

'See, I guide all things to the end that I planned for them before time began, and I do it with the same power and wisdom and love with which I made them. How should anything be amiss?' In this way, powerfully, wisely and lovingly, was my soul tested through this vision. Then I saw truly that I could do nothing else but assent to it with great reverence and joy in God.

(RDL ch.11)

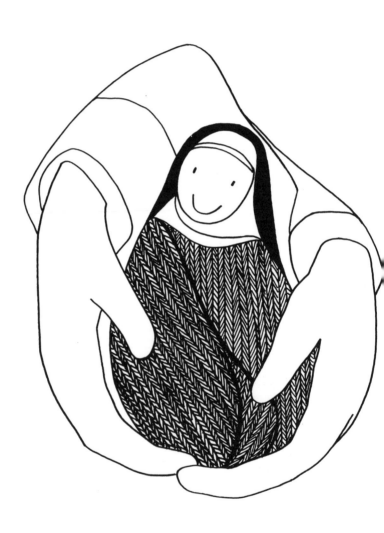

Always Kept Safe

After this God infused into my soul a most wonderful spiritual delight. I was completely filled with an awareness of everlasting security, in which I was powerfully sustained without any painful fear. This feeling was so glad and so spiritual that I was totally at peace, at ease and at rest, so that there was nothing on earth that could have grieved me.

This state lasted only for a short while, then all changed. I was left alone, deeply depressed and tired of life, so weary of myself that I could hardly bear to go on living. There was no comfort or calm for me now, only faith, hope and love; and these I did not feel, I only believed they were true.

Then soon after this our Blessed Lord once again gave me comfort and rest for my soul. This was so satisfying and certain, so blissfully happy and powerful, that no fear, no sorrow, no physical or spiritual pain of any kind could upset me. Then again I felt the pain, and then again the delight and joy. Now one, now the other, repeatedly, I suppose about twenty times. In the times of joy I could have said with St Paul: 'Nothing shall separate me from the love of Christ,' and in the pain I could have said with St Peter: 'Lord, save me, I am perishing.'

I understood that this vision was shown to teach me that it is good for some souls to feel like this, up in the air, then down in the dumps, sometimes strengthened, sometimes desolate and abandoned. God wants us to know that he keeps us always safe in bad and good times alike. And for the good of our soul we are sometimes left to ourselves, even though our sin may not always be the cause of it. For at this time I had committed no sin for which I should have been left to myself, it all happened too quickly. On the other hand, neither did I deserve these blissful feelings of joy. But our Lord gives freely whenever he wills, and sometimes he allows us to be in sorrow. Both are from one and same love. It is God's will that we do all in our power to stay in consolation, because bliss lasts for ever, while pain will pass and shall be brought to nothing for those who are going to be saved. Therefore it is not God's will that we dwell on the painful feelings and grieve and mourn over them. He wants us to pass them over quickly and keep ourselves in the endless delight which is God.

If there is anyone living on earth who is constantly being kept from falling into sin, I do not know, for it was not revealed to me. But it was revealed to me that whether in falling or in rising we are ever preciously protected in one love.

(*RDL* ch.15; ch.82:4)

Love and Compassion

Here I saw something of the compassion of our Lady St
Mary, for Christ and she were so one in love that the
greatness of her love was the cause of the greatness of
her pain. In this I saw the substance of natural love,
developed by grace, which his creatures have for him.
This natural love was most supremely and surpassingly
shown in his sweet mother. For as much as she loved him
more than all others, her pain surpassed all others. For
always the higher, the stronger, the sweeter love is, the
greater is the sorrow of one who sees the body of a
beloved suffer. So all his disciples and all his true lovers
suffered far more when he suffered than when they
themselves died. I am sure, from the way I feel myself,
that the very least of them loved him so much more than
they loved themselves that I am unable to put it into
words.

In this way I saw our Lord Jesus lingering for a long
time, because his union with the Godhead gave his
humanity strength to suffer more for love than the whole
of humankind could suffer. I mean, not only more pain

than anyone on earth could suffer; but also that he suffered more pain than all people together who will ever be saved (from the beginning of time to the very last day) could ever describe or imagine. Consider the worthiness of the most high, and that he the most worthy of all was most fully reduced to nothing and most utterly despised. Now the most important point that we have to consider in his Passion is to think and to register in our mind that he who suffered is God, and then reflect still on these other two points which are less important: one is *what* he suffered and the other is *for whom* he suffered.

In this vision he brought to my mind something of the sublimity and the nobility of the glorious Godhead, and at the same time the preciousness and tenderness of his blessed body which is united to it, and also the loathing that our nature experiences when confronted with pain. For just as he was the most tender and most pure of all people, so he was the one who suffered most deeply and intensely. He suffered for the sins of everyone that shall be saved. And he saw and grieved for everyone's sorrow, desolation and anguish out of kindness and love. For just as our Lady grieved for his suffering, so he also grieved for her suffering, indeed much more, since his sweet manhood was much nobler in nature. As long as he was capable of suffering, he suffered for us and grieved for us. Now he has risen again and so can no longer suffer. Yet he still suffers with us as I shall explain later. And as I, by his grace, contemplated all this, I saw that the love in him which he has for our souls was so strong that he chose to suffer deliberately, indeed, with a great desire, and he endured all the suffering gently and joyfully.

When a soul touched by grace looks at it like this, it shall truly see that the pains of Christ's Passion surpass all other pains; that is, all pains which will be turned into everlasting and supreme joy by the power of Christ's Passion.

(RDL ch.18:1; ch.20:1-3)

Choosing Jesus

At this time I wanted to look away from the Cross, but I dared not, because I knew quite well that while I gazed at the Cross I was secure and safe. Therefore I did not want to give in to the desire and put my soul in danger, for apart from the Cross there was no safety from the terror of demons.

Then a suggestion came to my mind in an apparently friendly manner: 'Look up to heaven to his Father.' With the faith I had I saw clearly that there was nothing between the cross and heaven that could have harmed me. I had therefore either to look up or else refuse to do so. I answered inwardly with all the power of my soul saying: 'No, I cannot, for you are my heaven.' I said this because I did not want to look up. I would rather have remained in that pain until Judgement Day than enter heaven in any other way than through him. I knew very well that he who bound me so painfully would unbind me when he wished.

In this way I was taught to choose Jesus for my heaven, whom I saw only in pain at that time. I wanted no other heaven than Jesus, who will be my bliss when I get there. It has always been a great comfort to me that by his grace I chose Jesus to be my heaven throughout all this time of his Passion and sorrow. This has taught me that I should always do so, choosing only·Jesus to be my heaven through thick and thin.

(*RDL* ch.19:1–3)

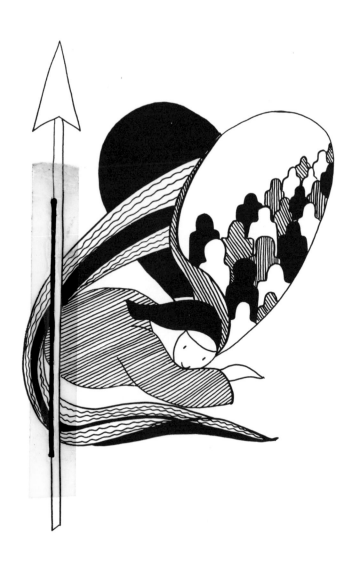

The Heart of Christ

With a joyful expression our Good Lord looked at his wounded side and contemplated it with joy; and with his sweet gaze he led the understanding of this creature through the same wound into his side, right inside it. And there he showed me a beautiful and enjoyable place, big enough to contain all humankind that shall be saved that they might rest there in peace and in love. And with this he brought to my mind his priceless blood and the precious water which he allowed to flow out for love of us. In this sweet contemplation he showed his blessed heart cloven in two; and with great delight he showed to my understanding, partially, the blessed Godhead (as far as he wanted at that moment), strengthening in this way the poor soul to understand that which was without beginning, and is, and ever shall be.

And with this our Good Lord said most blissfully: 'See how much I love you!' as if he had said: 'My dear one, behold and see your Lord, your God, who is your creator and your endless joy. See your own brother, your Saviour. My child, behold and see what delight and bliss

I have in your salvation, and for my love rejoice now with me.'

And further, in order to have a still deeper understanding, this blessed word was said: 'See how much I love you!' It was as if he had said: 'Behold and see that I loved you so much before I died for you, that I was willing to die for you. Now I have died for you and suffered willingly what I could, and now all my bitter pains and all my hard turmoil have changed into endless joy and bliss for me and for you. How should it now be that you should ask me for anything that pleases me and I should not give it you with pleasure? For my pleasure is your holiness and your endless joy and bliss with me.'

This is the understanding, as simply as I can put it, of this blessed word: 'See how much I love you.' This has been shown to me by our good Lord in order to make us glad and happy.

The human mother can put her child tenderly to her breast, but our tender mother, Jesus, can lead us intimately into his blessed breast, through the sweet open wound in his side, and there give us a glimpse of the Godhead and the joy of heaven, with the inner certainty of eternal bliss. He revealed this in the tenth Revelation, making it clear to me with these sweet words: 'See, how I love you,' as I contemplated his blessed side, rejoicing over it.

(*RDL* ch.24; ch.60:6)

It Is I

And after this our Lord showed himself more glorified than I had ever seen him before. By this I was taught that our soul will never have rest until it comes to him, knowing that he is full of joy, homely and courteous, full of bliss and true life. Our Lord Jesus repeatedly said:

'It is I, it is I.
It is I who am highest.
It is I whom you love.
It is I in whom you rejoice.
It is I whom you serve.
It is I for whom you long.
It is I whom you desire.
It is I whom you mean.
It is I who am the all.
It is I whom Holy Church preaches and teaches to
         you.
It is I who showed himself to you before.'

The number of the words surpass my will and my understanding and all my powers. And they were most sublime, as far as I could see, for in them is comprehended what I am unable to tell. But the joy which I saw in the revelation that was made to me about them surpasses all that the heart can think of or the soul may mean. And therefore these words are not being explained here, but may everyone, according to the grace which God gives each in intelligence and love, receive them as intended by our Lord.

Let us flee to our Lord and we shall be comforted. Let us touch him and we shall be made clean. Let us cleave to him and we shall be secure and safe from every kind of harm. Our courteous Lord wants us to feel as at home with him as the heart can conceive or the soul desire. But let us be careful not to treat this close friendship so casually that we forget courtesy. For while our Lord is utter homeliness, he is as courteous as he is homely, for he is true courtesy. And he wants the blessed creatures, who will be in heaven with him for ever, to be like him in all things; for to be exactly like our Lord is our true salvation and our greatest bliss. If we do not know how we shall do all this, then let us request it from our Lord, and he will teach us, for it is his delight and his glory; blessed may he be!

When we have fallen through frailty or blindness, then our courteous Lord raises us up with his gentle touch and protects us. He wants us to see how wretched we are and humbly face up to it. But he does not want us to stay like that, or to be preoccupied with self-accusation or to wallow in self-pity. But he wants us quickly to attend to him, for he stands all alone, and he is always waiting for us, sorrowing and grieving until we come. He hurries to bring us back to him, for we are his joy and his delight, and he is our salvation and our life.

(RDL ch.26:1,2; ch.77:7; ch.79:5)

Compassion towards One Another

I saw how Christ has compassion on us because of sin. And just as I was before full of pain and compassion because of the Passion of Christ, so I was now full of compassion for all my fellow-Christians.

Yes, I saw clearly that our Lord even rejoices with pity and compassion over the tribulations of his servants. And on each person whom he loves and wants to bring to his bliss, he lays something that in his eyes is not a defect yet makes them to be humiliated, despised, scorned, mocked and rejected in this world. And this he does to prevent them from being harmed by the pomp, the pride and the vainglory of this wretched life, and to prepare them better for the way that will bring them to heaven with infinite joy and eternal bliss. For he says: 'I shall completely break you from your empty affections and from your vicious pride, and then I shall gather you together and make you humble and gentle, pure and holy through one-ing you to me.'

And then I saw that every natural compassion that anyone has for a fellow-Christian is due to Christ living within.

I could not see any kind of anger in God, neither short-lived nor long-lasting. For truly, as I see it, if God were angry even for a moment, we could neither have life, nor place, nor being. As truly as we have our being from the eternal power of God and from the eternal wisdom and from the eternal goodness, just as truly we have our safe keeping in the eternal power of God, in the eternal wisdom and in the eternal goodness. Though we may feel in ourselves anger, disagreement and strife, yet we are all mercifully enfolded in God's mildness and humility, in his kindness and graciousness.

I saw very clearly that all our everlasting friendship, our home, our life and our being are in God. The same everlasting goodness that keeps hold of us when we sin so that we do not perish, that same everlasting goodness continually gives us peace instead of all our anger and our perverse feeling.

(RDL ch.28:1a,2,3a; ch.49:2,3)

Pondering on Sin

After this our Lord brought to my mind the longing I had for him earlier, and I saw that nothing hindered me except sin. This I saw to be true in general for all of us. And I thought to myself: 'If there had been no sin, we should all have been pure and clean like our Lord, as he created us.' And so in my foolishness, before this time, I had often wondered why God with his great foresight and wisdom did not prevent the beginning of sin in the first place. For then, I thought, all would have been well.

This curious wondering would have been better left alone, but instead, I mourned and sorrowed over it without reason and discretion. But Jesus, who in this vision instructed me in everything that I needed to know, answered me with this word and said: 'Sin is necessary, but all shall be well, and all shall be well, and all manner of things shall be well.'

By this bare word 'sin' our Lord meant me to understand in general all that is not good. It includes the shameful contempt and the uttermost tribulation that our Lord endured for us in this life, his death with all his pains, and the suffering of all his creatures both in spirit and in the body. For all of us are at times distressed and we shall continue to be so (like Jesus our Master) until we are wholly purified in our mortal flesh and in all our interior affections that are not wholly good.

And in this sight with all the pains that ever were or ever shall be, I understood the Passion of Christ to be the greatest pain, far surpassing them all. All this was shown to me in an instant of time and quickly passed over into comfort. For our good Lord did not want the soul to be frightened by this ugly sight. But 'sin' itself I did not see, because I believe that it does not have its own substance or any form of being, nor can it be known except by the pain it causes.

It seems to me that this pain is something very real and it lasts for a while, because it purifies us, makes us know ourselves, and ask for mercy. But the Passion of our Lord is a comfort to us in all this, and this is his blessed will. Because of the tender love that our Lord has for those who shall be saved, he gives comfort quickly and sweetly, his meaning being: 'Yes, it is true, sin is the root and cause of all pain, but all shall be well, and all manner of things shall be well.'

These words were revealed to me most tenderly, without any kind of blame either towards me or anybody else who shall be saved. It would therefore indeed be unbecoming of me to blame God or question him about my sin, since he does not blame me for it.

And in these same words I saw a wonderful and most

profound mystery hidden in God, which will be clearly made known to us in heaven. When we shall know this mystery, then we shall truly know why he allowed sin to come, and knowing that, we shall rejoice in him for ever.

(*RDL* ch.27)

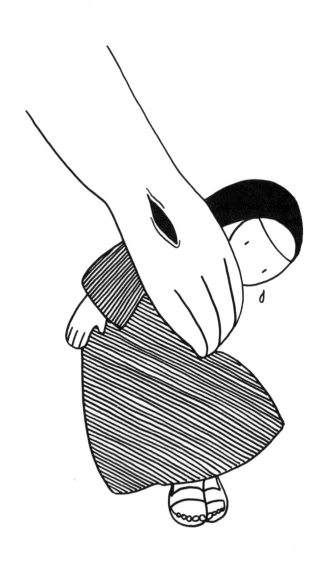

When We Sin

It is a sign of the supreme friendship of our courteous Lord that he should keep hold of us so tenderly while we are in our sin. Furthermore he touches us most secretly and shows us our sin in the sweet light of his mercy and grace. But when we see ourselves so foul, then we think that God should be angry with us for our sin. Then we are inspired by the Holy Spirit by means of contrition to pray and to desire with all our might to amend our life, in order to still God's anger until we are able to find rest of soul and peace of conscience. Then we hope that God has forgiven us our sin and he really has. Our courteous Lord then shows himself to the soul with a joyful and happy expression and in a friendly welcoming way, as if the soul had come out of imprisonment and suffering, saying: 'My darling, I am glad that you have come to me. I have always been with you in all your troubles, and now you see me loving and we are made one in bliss.'

This is how sins are forgiven by grace and mercy, and our soul honourably and joyfully received just as it will be when it comes to heaven. This happens whenever the soul experiences the gracious working of the Holy Spirit and the power of Christ's Passion.

Here I understood truly that all kinds of things are prepared for us by the great goodness of God, so much so that when we ourselves are in peace and in love, we are truly safe. But because we cannot have this in its fullness whilst we are here, it is necessary for us always to live with our Lord Jesus in sweet prayer and love-filled longing.

And if we, through our blindness and wretchedness ever fall, let us quickly get up, being aware of the sweet touching of grace, and willingly amend ourselves according to the teaching of Holy Church and in accordance with the seriousness of the sin. Then we continue our way with God in love, neither on the one hand belittling ourselves so much that we fall into despair, nor on the other hand living so recklessly as if we did not care a thing. Rather, we ought humbly to recognize our weakness, admit that we cannot stand on our own feet even for a twinkling of an eye, without the help of grace, and reverently cling to God, trusting only in him.

(*RDL* ch.40:1–3a; ch.52:7)

Teaching on Prayer

Our Lord showed me teaching about prayer. In this revelation I saw that the Lord had in mind two conditions: one is rightful prayer and the other absolute trust. Yet often our trust is half-hearted, because we are not sure that God hears us. This is because we think we are not good enough and because we feel nothing at all, for often we are as barren and dry after our prayers as we were before. And so when we are in such a state of mind, our foolishness becomes the cause of our weakness in prayer. I have experienced this myself.

Praying is a true, gracious and lasting will of the soul, united and fastened to the will of our Lord by the sweet inner work of the Holy Spirit. Our Lord himself is the first to receive our prayer, as I see it, and he accepts it with great thankfulness; and with great rejoicing, he raises it up and places it in his treasure-house where it will never perish. It is there before God with all his holy saints, constantly accepted, ever furthering our cause. And when we shall receive our bliss, our prayer will be given back to us as an extra joy with endless praise and thanks from him.

Our Lord is very happy and glad with our prayer. He expects it and he wants to have it, because with his grace it makes us like himself in condition as we are in nature. This is his blessed will, for he says: 'Pray wholeheartedly, even though you don't feel like it, for it is a very profitable thing to do, even if you don't feel that way. Pray wholeheartedly, even when you may feel nothing, even when you see nothing, yes, even when you think you cannot do it. For in times of dryness and barrenness, in times of sickness and weakness, your prayer is most pleasing to me, even though you may find it rather tasteless. And this holds good in my eyes for all your prayers said in faith.'

Because of the reward and the endless thanks which he wants to give, he desires to have us constantly praying before him. God accepts the good intentions and the effort of his servants, regardless of our feelings. Therefore it pleases him to see us at work both in prayer and in good living with his help and grace, directing all our faculties to him intelligently and with discretion, until we possess in complete joy the one we seek, Jesus himself.

To centre on the goodness of God is the highest form of prayer, and God's goodness comes to meet us at our most basic need. It gives life to our soul and makes it live and grow in grace and virtue. It is the nearest to us by nature and the readiest to bring us grace, for it is the same grace that the soul seeks and ever will, until the day in which we truly know God who has completely enfolded us all in himself.

Thanksgiving is also an integral part of prayer. Thanksgiving is a true inward awareness. With deep reverence and loving fear it leads us to turn with all our strength to the work the Lord is calling us to do, all the time rejoicing and thanking him in our hearts. Sometimes the soul is so full that it overflows into words and cries out: 'Good Lord, thanks be to you, may you be blessed.' And sometimes when the heart is dry and feels nothing, or else, when attacked by an enemy, then reason and grace drive us to cry out aloud to our Lord, recounting his blessed Passion and his great goodness. Then the power of our Lord's word enters the soul and enlivens the heart, leading it by his grace into true working, causing it to pray with utter happiness, and truly to delight in our Lord. This is for him a most loving thanksgiving.

(*RDL* ch.41:1a,3-5; ch.6:4; ch.41:6)

Mercy And Grace

The ground of mercy is love, and the work of mercy is to keep us safe in love. This was shown in such a way that I could not perceive the property of mercy in any other way than as it were all love in love.

This means (as far as I can see) that mercy is sweet, gracious, working in love, mingled with abundant pity. For mercy is at work protecting us, and mercy is at work transforming everything into good for us. Mercy, out of love, allows us to fall to a certain extent. And to the extent that we fail we fall, and to the extent that we fall we die. We must necessarily die in as much as we fail to see and feel God, who is our life. Our failing is dreadful, our falling is shameful, and our dying is sorrowful. Yet in all this the sweet eye of pity and love never turns away from us, and the work of mercy never fails.

I contemplated the property of mercy and I contemplated the property of grace. Both work differently in one and the same love. Mercy is a property full of compassion, which belongs to motherhood in tender love. Grace is a property full of glory which belongs to royal lordship in the same love. Mercy works thus: protecting, enduring, bringing life and healing, and all is from the tenderness of love. Grace works with mercy: bringing up, rewarding, endlessly exceeding everything that our loving and labour deserve; spreading, spreading forth widely and showing the noble and abundant generosity of God's royal lordship in his marvellous courtesy. And this is from the abundance of love, for grace transforms our dreadful failing into plentiful and endless consolation. And grace transforms our shameful falling into a high and glorious rising. And grace transforms our sorrowful dying into a holy and blissful life.

(*RDL* ch.48:2–4)

God Our Peace

Although our blindness and weakness have allowed the anger and rebellion that is in us to lead us into hardship, distress and suffering, yet we are kept perfectly safe by God's merciful protection, so that we do not perish. But we shall not be blissfully safe and in possession of our endless joy until we are wholly in peace and in love; that is to say fully content with God, and with all his actions and decisions, and at peace and in love with ourselves, with our fellow-Christians and with all that God loves, as is pleasing to love. It is God's goodness that brings this about in us.

So I saw that God is our true peace, and he is our sure protector when we ourselves are not at peace, and he constantly works to bring us into everlasting peace. So when by the working of mercy and grace we are made humble and gentle, then shall we be fully safe. When the soul is truly at peace with itself, then it is at once united to God, because in him there is no anger. So I saw that when we are wholly in peace and in love, we find no opposition or any kind of hindrance in us; in fact, our

Lord God in his goodness turns all the opposition that is now in us to our advantage.

Let us desire then of our Lord God the gift to fear him reverently, love him meekly and trust him with all our strength, for when we fear him reverently, love him meekly, our trust is never in vain. For the more we trust him and the stronger our trust is, the more we please and glorify our Lord in whom we trust. If we fail to offer God this reverent fear and humble love (and God forbid that we should!) our trust will, while that lasts, soon go all wrong. So we very much need to pray to our Lord for grace that we may have the gift of reverent fear and meek love in our hearts and in our work, for without this no one can please God.

(RDL ch.49:5,6; ch.74:8)

A Parable

I saw two persons in bodily likeness, that is to say, a Lord
and a servant. With this God gave me a spiritual understanding. The Lord is sitting in state, quietly and
peacefully. The servant is standing before him, respect-
fully, ready to do his Lord's will. The Lord looks at his
servant most lovingly and tenderly, and gently he sends
him to a certain place to do his will. The servant not only
goes, but jumps up at once and races off, driven by love,
to do his Lord's will. But suddenly he falls into a pit and
is badly injured, then he groans and moans, tosses about
and struggles, but he cannot get up or help himself in any
way. In all this, the greatest hurt that I saw in him was
the lack of comfort, because he was unable to turn his
face to look at his loving Lord who was very close to him,
and who had all the comfort he needs. But like a man
who was feeble and foolish for a moment, he focused his
attention on his feelings and on his continuing distress.

In this distress he suffered seven great pains. The first
was the severe bruising that he took in his falling, which
gave him great pain. The second was the sluggishness of

his body. The third was the weakness that resulted from these two pains. The fourth was that he was confused in his thinking and his mind was in such a state of shock that he had almost forgotten his own love. The fifth was that he could not get up. The sixth was the most astonishing pain to me, namely, that he lay totally alone; I looked all around and searched, I looked far and near, high and low, but could see no help for him. The seventh was that the place in which he lay was narrow, hard and painful.

I wondered how this servant could endure all this suffering with such humility. I looked very carefully to see whether I could find any fault in him, or whether the Lord would attribute any kind of blame to him, and truly I saw none, for the only cause of his falling was his good will and his great desire. In his spirit he was still as keen and as good as when he stood before his Lord, ready to do his will. That is how his loving Lord continually looked at him most tenderly.

In the servant there is a double meaning: one outward, the other inward. Outwardly he was dressed simply, like a workman ready to do hard work, and he stood very near to the Lord – not straight in front of him, but slightly to one side and that to the left. He was wearing a single white tunic, old and shapeless, stained with the sweat of his body, tight-fitting and short, as it were, barely a hand's width below his knee. It looked threadbare as if it would soon be worn out it was so ragged and torn. I was greatly surprised by this, thinking, 'What unsuitable clothing for a servant who is so much loved to wear in front of such a great Lord.'

But inwardly, I saw in him a ground of love. The love which he had for his Lord and which was equal to the love that the Lord had for him.

By the closeness of the servant is understood the Son, and by the standing on the left side is understood Adam. The Lord is God the Father. The servant is the Son, Jesus Christ. The Holy Spirit is the love which is in them both equally.

When Adam fell, God's Son fell, because in their true and heaven-made union, God's Son could not be separated from Adam, for by Adam is understood all humanity. Adam fell from life to death, into the depths of this wretched world, and then into hell. God's Son fell with Adam into the depths of the virgin's womb who was the fairest daughter of Adam, in order to rescue Adam from all blame in heaven and on earth. Then with wonderful power he brought him out of hell.

By the wisdom and goodness that was in the servant is understood God's Son. By the poor clothing as a workman and the standing close by on the left is understood Adam's humanity with all the harm and weakness that follow from that. For in all this our good Lord showed his own Son and Adam as only one man. The strength and goodness that we have is from Jesus Christ, and weakness and blindness that we have is from Adam. Both were shown in the one servant.

Thus our good Lord Jesus has taken upon himself all our blame and therefore our Father may not and will not assign more blame to us than to his own beloved Son Jesus Christ. So he was the servant before he came to earth standing ready before his Father willing to carry out his will, until such time when he could be sent to do the glorious work which would bring humankind back to heaven. That is to say, even though he is God, equal with his Father in his divinity, yet because he knew his future purpose to become man in order to save humankind in obedience to his Father's will, he stood before his Father as a servant willing to be charged with all the responsibility for us. Then eagerly he rushed off at the Father's bidding, without sparing a thought for himself or his harsh pains, and soon fell right down into the virgin's womb.

Now the Lord no longer sits on the ground in the wilderness, but he sits on his rich and noble seat which he made in heaven most to his liking. Now the Son does not stand before the Father as a servant before the Lord poorly clothed, half-naked, but he stands now right in front of the Father, richly and lavishly dressed, with a rich and priceless crown on his head. It was revealed to me that we are his crown, and that this crown is the Father's joy, the Son's glory, the Holy Spirit's delight, and the endless marvellous bliss to all who are in heaven.

(*RDL* ch.51 [with omissions])

Christ Is Our Mother

Because he wanted to become wholly our mother in all things, our mother in nature (who is also our mother in grace) began his work in complete humility and gentleness, in the Virgin's womb. He revealed this in the first Revelation when he brought that gentle virgin before my mind's eyes in the simple condition in which she found herself when she conceived.

That is to say, in this humble place, our great God, the supreme wisdom of all things, arrayed himself in our poor flesh and fully prepared himself to do the work and service of motherhood in all things. The service of the mother is nearest, readiest and most reliable. Its nearness is because it is most natural, its readiness is because it is most loving, and its reliability is because it is most true. No one might or ever could perform this office perfectly, except him alone. We know that our mothers bear us for pain and for death. But what is it that Jesus, our true mother, does? He who is all-love bears us for joy and eternal life. Blessed may he be! So he sustained us and carried us within him in love and in labour until the fullness of time, when he wanted to suffer the sharpest thorns and the most cruel pains that have ever been and ever shall be, until at the end he died. And when he had finished and had given birth to us for bliss, even then his most wonderful love was not satisfied, as he revealed in these high, surpassing words of love. 'If I could suffer more I would suffer more.'

He could not die any more but he would not cease working. So he had to feed us, for the most precious love of motherhood has placed this obligation towards us upon him. The human mother suckles her child with her own milk, but our precious mother Jesus can feed us with himself, and he does this most constantly and tenderly by means of the Blessed Sacrament, which is the precious food of true life.

Jesus feeds us and helps us, just as the high sovereign nature of motherhood demands, and as the maternal need of childhood requires. Fair and sweet is our heavenly Mother in the eyes of our soul, precious and loving are the grace-filled children in the eyes of the homely Mother, with the gentleness and meekness and all the lovely virtues which belong to children by nature. For naturally the child does not rely on itself, and naturally the child loves its mother, as the mother loves the child.

These are the beautiful virtues which, together with all the others that are like them, serve and please our heavenly Mother. I saw that in this life there is no state greater in weakness and in lack of power and intelligence than the one of childhood, until the day when our mother of grace brings us up into our Father's bliss. And there it shall be made known to us what he means by these sweet words: 'All shall be well; and you shall see for yourself that all manner of things shall be well.' Then the bliss of our motherhood in Christ will begin anew in the joys of God our Father, and this new beginning shall continue being renewed without end.

So I understand that all his blessed children who have been born of him by nature shall be brought back to him by grace.

Our Father wills, our Mother works, our Lord the Holy Spirit confirms. Therefore we must love our God in whom we have our being. We must reverently thank and praise him for creating us, fervently praying to our Mother for mercy and compassion and to our Lord the Holy Spirit for help and grace. For in these three is all our life: nature, mercy and grace. From these we have gentleness, patience, pity and hatred of sin and wickedness, for it is in the nature of virtue to hate sin and wickedness.

So Jesus is our true mother in nature through creating us in the first place, and he is our true mother in grace through taking on our created nature. All the loving service and all the sweet and gentle offices of precious motherhood are proper to the Second Person, for in him we have this 'godly will' whole and safe for ever, both in nature and in grace, by his own innate goodness.

So our life is grounded in Jesus, our true Mother, in his own foreseeing wisdom without a beginning, together with the almighty power of the Father and the supreme goodness of the Holy Spirit. By taking our nature he gave us life, and in the blessed dying on the Cross he brought us forth to eternal life.

(*RDL* ch.60:2-4; ch.63:5-7; ch.59:4,5; ch.63:4)

Persevering In Joy And Trust

I understood that any man or woman who freely chooses God in this life for love's sake can be sure of being eternally loved with the eternal love that produces in him this grace. God wants us trustfully to believe in this truth: that is, that we are as certain in our hope of the eternal bliss of heaven whilst we are here as we shall be certain to possess it when we are there.

And the more delight and joy we take in this certainty, with reverence and humility, the more we please him. This is what was shown to me. This reverence that I am speaking of is a holy and respectful fear of our Lord to which humility is knit. This means that a creature sees the Lord as amazingly great and self as amazingly small. These virtues are the eternal possession of those whom God loves. This can even now be seen and felt to some degree when our Lord is present with his grace. This presence in all things is very much desired because it creates that wonderful sense of security in true faith and in certain hope that comes from a very great love, together with a sweet and delightful fear.

It is God's will that I should see myself as duty-bound to him in love as if all he had ever done he has done for me.

Our good Lord showed himself to his creatures in various ways, both in heaven and on earth, but the only place in which I saw him actually take up residence was in the human soul.

He revealed himself on earth in his sweet Incarnation and in his blessed Passion. He also revealed himself in other ways on earth, for instance where I said: 'I saw God in one point.' Then he showed himself in another way here on earth as if he were on pilgrimage: that is to say, that he is here with us, leading us, and staying with us till he has brought us all to his bliss in heaven.

He revealed himself several times residing, as I have said, chiefly in the human soul. He has made our soul his resting place and his royal city. And from this glorious throne he will never ever get up or move away permanently.

The place where the Lord dwells is wonderful and magnificent, and therefore he wants us to respond quickly to the touch of his grace, rejoicing more in his unbroken love than sorrowing over our frequent falls. For out of all the things that we can do, the one that gives him most honour is to live gladly and joyfully for love of him.

(*RDL* ch.65:1,2; ch.81:1–4)

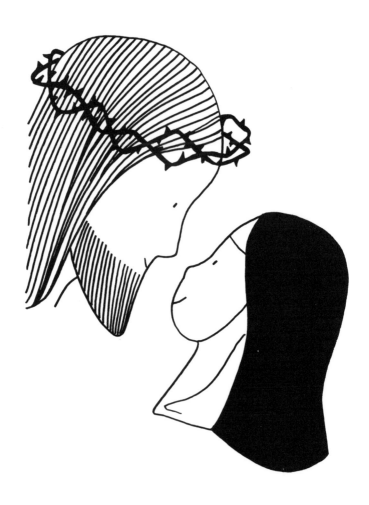

The Face of Christ

Glad and joyful and sweet is the blessed and lovely expression that our Lord shows to our souls, for he sees us always living in love-longing, and he wants our souls to turn cheerfully to him in order to give him his reward. And so I hope that with his grace he has and will evermore draw our outer expression to conform with our inner expression and so make us all one with him and with each other in that true eternal joy which is Jesus.

I see in our Lord's face three kinds of expression. The first is the expression of the Passion as he showed it when he was with us in this life at the time of death. And although this sight is mournful and sorrowful, yet it remains glad and joyful because he is God. The second expression is pity, tenderness and compassion. This he shows to all his lovers with the assurance of complete protection for those who are in need of his mercy.

The third expression is that blessed face as it shall be

without end. This was shown most often and continued for the longest period of time.

And so when we are in pain and distress he reveals to us the face of his Passion and his Cross, helping us to bear ours with his own blessed power. And when we sin he shows us the expression of pity and compassion powerfully protecting and defending us against all our enemies. These are the two usual expressions that he shows us in this life. Mixed with them is the third, namely that blessed face, partially like what it will be in heaven. This comes about by the touch of grace and the sweet enlightenment of the spiritual life, through which we are kept in true faith, hope and love, in contrition and in devotion, as well as in contemplation and in all the different kinds of true joy and sweet consolations. The blessed face of God our Lord does all this in us through his grace.

He will never have full joy in us until we have full joy in him, seeing in reality his fair blessed face. For we are destined for this by nature and brought to it by grace. So I saw how sin is for a short while deadly to the blessed creatures destined for eternal life.

And ever the more clearly that the soul sees this blessed face by the grace of loving, the more it yearns to see it in fullness, that is, in his true likeness. For even though our Lord God dwells now in us, and is here with us, though he calls us and enfolds us out of his tender love so that he can never leave us, though he is nearer to us than tongue can tell or heart can thirst, yet we can never cease mourning and weeping, nor seeking or longing, until we can clearly look at him in his blessed face. In that precious blessed sight there can be no more grief nor any lack of well-being.

(RDL ch.71:2-4; ch.72:2b,3)

All Shall Be Well

On one occasion our good Lord said: 'All manner of things shall be well.' And on another occasion he said: 'You shall see for yourself that all manner of things shall be well.' And from these two statements the soul took various meanings. One meaning is that he wants us to know that he takes care not only of the noble and great things, but also of the humble and small, the lowly and simple things, both of the one and the other. This is what he means when he says: 'All manner of things shall be well.' For he wants us to know that even the least things shall not be forgotten.

Another meaning is that there are many deeds being done which in our eyes are so evil and lead to so much harm that it seems to us impossible that any good can ever come out of them. And we cannot be quiet and rest in the blessed contemplation of God as we should, because we dwell on all this evil, and sorrow and grieve over it. And the cause of it is that our mind is now so blind, so feeble and so foolish that we are unable to recognize the supreme and wonderful wisdom, power and goodness of the blessed Trinity. And this is what he means when he says: 'You shall see for yourself that all manner of things shall be well.' It is as if he said: 'Accept it now in faith and in trust, and at the end you will see it as it really is in complete joy.'

In spite of our foolish living and our blindness here on earth, our courteous Lord is always looking at us, rejoicing in this work in us. And of all things, we can please him best by wisely and sincerely believing this and by rejoicing with him and in him. For as truly as we shall be in the bliss of God without end, praising him and thanking him, so truly have we been in the foresight of God, loved and known in his eternal plan from without beginning. In this love without beginning he made us, and in this same love he protects us, and never allows us to be hurt in any way by which our bliss might be diminished.

When the judgement is given and we are all brought up above, then we shall clearly see in God the mysteries which are now hidden from us. Then none of us will have the slightest urge to say: 'Lord, if it had been like this, it would have been fine.' Instead we shall all say with one voice: 'Lord, blessed may you be, because it is like this: all is well. Now we can truly see that everything has been done just as you planned it before anything was made.'

(RDL ch.32:1,2; ch.85:1,2)

Epilogue

After Julian's death her cell was occupied by a succession of anchoresses until the Reformation, when it was demolished and the monastic buildings of Norfolk despoiled.

And her book? Unlike most of the continental mystics Julian belonged to no Order which might cherish her memory and disseminate her writings. Nor had she a devout following, such as the 'spiritual sons' of Angela of Foligno or the 'Caterinati' who surrounded Catherine of Siena. She was not known as an ecstatic or mystic to the general populace. Her life within the anchorhold was similar to that of any other woman solitary. There were no levitations, no further visions, no inspired heavenly pronouncements – she was a pragmatic, down-to-earth Englishwoman. Her *Shewings* were behind her and she spent a lifetime meditating on them. She or a scribe had recorded her deepening understanding of what she had 'seen' as she lay near death. But for the rest of her life she had to live, like all Christians, by dark faith – praying, pondering, questioning, sifting, penetrating the mystery of Christ and his redeeming work.

Julian's book would be written by hand, a time-consuming task, and it would not be the kind of work to merit valuable illumination or precious materials. It was in English, not Latin, its author was an unknown recluse, and the majority of copies available were no doubt destroyed when the monasteries were dissolved.

But one copy found its way to the Bibliothèque Nationale in Paris. From this version it is presumed that Serenus de Cressy, a Benedictine monk living on the continent, published the first edition of Julian's work in 1670. Two other manuscripts were discovered much later among the Sloane collection of books at the British Museum. One of these manuscripts was edited and published in England in 1877 by Henry Collins, who had previously, under the pseudonym of 'A Secular Priest' translated and edited *The Visions and Instructions of Angela of Foligno*. In his Introduction to this book he speaks of his coming project on Julian, citing her as Angela's English equal. Today, Angela is scarcely read; it is Julian who proves to be of greater stature and contemporary appeal.

However, these earlier editions of Julian's *Revelations* had few readers; English Catholic spirituality from pre-Reformation times was mostly unexplored territory. But in 1901 a previously unknown and self-taught scholar, Grace Warrack, brought out a new edition which quickly attained great popularity. Suddenly people awoke to the fact that here was a woman who had something to say to the twentieth century, and many translations, commentaries and popular expositions of Julian and her teaching have followed. She even has an Order named after her in the USA's Episcopalian Church.

A shorter version of the *Revelations* came to light in 1909 when an anthology of Catholic devotions was bought by the British Museum from the library of Lord Amherst, member of an old Catholic family. This unique document was first thought to be an abridged version of the full book, but scholars now agree it was written first, soon after Julian's visions and before she had had time to ponder their contents as fully as she did twenty years later in the longer book.

Julian seems to have been 'kept' for today, fresh and inspiring, a voice of joy and optimism, yet also a powerful prober of life's ultimate questions. She is a true searcher after God, fully committed to him and to others; original in her thinking, traditional in her Christian devotion, courageous in exploring, stable in her radical commitment to solitude – a solitude in which she held, with love, all her fellow-Christians. From being voiceless and unknown, Julian is now acclaimed. Thomas Merton, the well-known Cistercian monk, admitted that he would prefer Julian to St John of the Cross, calling her, together with Newman, the greatest theologian England has produced. It is this theological approach which appeals, a theology rooted in life and daily experience. Julian is not a mere 'descriptive visionary'; she really penetrates the *meaning* of the Christian mystery and elucidates it in an inimitable and original way.

Today another cell has been built on the site of Julian's anchorhold. It is a place of silence, of prayer, devoid of clutter. Here one is invited to enter, with her, into the wonder of being loved by God.

What Julian experienced was, she knew, not for herself alone. Her book, as she says, is to be taken as a personal revelation of the love God bears to each one who reads it.

And you, who shall get hold of this book, thank our Lord Jesus Christ generously and whole-heartedly for having made these visions and revelations to you and for you out of his endless love, mercy and goodness, to be for you and for all of us a safe guide and conduct to everlasting bliss. May Jesus grant us this. Amen.

Here ends the sublime and wonderful revelations of the unutterable love of God in Jesus Christ, vouchsafed to a dear lover of his, and in her to all his dear friends and lovers, whose hearts, like hers, do flame in the love of our dearest Jesus.

Bibliography and Further Reading

General Background

Bro. Arnold, *Visions and Instructions of Bl. Angela of Foligno*,
    translated by a Secular Priest (Richardson, 1871)
Irene Claremont de Castillejo, *Knowing Woman* (Harper
    Colophon, 1973)
Julian Celebration Committee, *Julian's Norwich* (1973)
David Knowles, *The English Mystical Tradition* (Burns and
    Oates, 1961)
K. Leech and B. Ward, *Julian Reconsidered* (SLG Press,
    1988)
Sheila Upjohn, *Who was Julian of Norwich?* (Darton,
    Longman and Todd, 1990)

Julian Studies

Ritamary Bradly, *Julian's Way* (HarperCollins, 1992)
R. Llewelyn (ed.), *Julian, Woman of our Day* (Darton,
    Longman and Todd, 1985)

R. Llewelyn, *With Pity not with Blame* (Darton, Longman and Todd, 1982)

John M. Mountney, *Sin shall be Glory* (Darton, Longman and Todd, 1992)

Brant Pelphrey, *Christ our Mother* (Darton, Longman and Todd, 1989)

Brant Pelphrey, *Love was his Meaning: the theology and mysticism of Julian of Norwich* (Salzburg University, 1982)

Devotional

Austin Cooper, OMI, *Julian of Norwich: Reflections on Selected Texts* (Burns and Oates, 1987)

R. Llewelyn (ed.), *Enfolded in Love: daily readings with Julian of Norwich* (Darton, Longman and Todd, 1980)

Texts

Julian of Norwich, *A Lesson of Love: the Revelations of Julian of Norwich*, edited and translated by John Julian, OJN (Darton, Longman and Todd, 1988)

Julian of Norwich, *Revelations of Divine Love*, translated and with an introduction by Clifton Wolters (Penguin, 1966)

Julian of Norwich, *A Shewing of God's Love* (shorter version), edited by Anna Maria Reynolds (Longmans Green, 1958)